Dislocations in Crystal

Michael Boughn

Dislocations in Crystal

Coach House Books

first edition

Published with the financial assistance of the Canada Council for the Arts
and the Ontario Arts Council

NATIONAL LIBRARY OF CANADA
CATALOGUING IN PUBLICATION DATA

Boughn, Michael
    Dislocations in crystal / Michael Boughn.

Poems.
ISBN 1-55245-111-9

    I. Title.

PS8553.O8342D58 2003   C811'.6   C2002-904845-1
PR9199.4.B67D58 2003

for Jack, with love

The growth of a crystal proceeds in response to changes in pressure and temperature, by steps, around nodes by shearing and twist. These deformations and dislocations give us the keys to ... the structural basis for the 'hereditary information transfer' which is the basis of life.

    – Muriel Ruykeyser, *The Traces of Thomas Hariot*

Art as such is what I wanted to achieve. We have not yet achieved it.

    – Joseph Beuys

The domestic man, who loves no music so well as the kitchen clock and the airs which the logs sing to him as they burn on the hearth has solaces which others never dream of.

    – Ralph Waldo Emerson, 'Prudence'

Some Fore-Words

THESE POEMS OPEN into the death of *Arabia Felix* (the
culture, not the place), the rise of Imperial Europe and even-
tually the tumult of these other empires in which we now
find ourselves entangled, all of it founded on Henry the
Navigator's relentless push to get around Africa on the way
to the Spice Islands. Not only did Henry's success bring an
end to the European caravans whose taxed wealth had
funded the flowering brilliance of medieval Arab culture
but, in the process, he also developed the instruments that
made possible Columbus's cataclysmic voyage across the
Atlantic. It all starts there, then: on Cape Espichel, just
south of the western extremity of Europe, just north of
Henry's school with its wind rose etched in stone, where at
the end of a canyon of centuries-old pilgrims' quarters in
utter decay, lie the ruins of Our Lady of the Cape. It is a
terrifying order of *terrain vague*, ill-defined and perched
between here and here, between now and now, where
syntax flutters back and forth, in and out of the knowable,
the measurable, honouring its dark ground without aban-
doning its promise. Adrift in history and myth, fairy tales
and TV, the tedious and the unexpected, the ordinary and
the marvellous, these poems seek a glimpse of unanticipated
forms and disparate knowledges in the detritus of experi-
ence piled up in the corners of the millennial turn, a land as
promised, not of the given but the taken. The poems cross
and recross untold regions of the heart disguised as a New
World, scattering the seeds of the yet-to-be-thought, drawn
on by a dream past apocalypse.

Prelude: Ode to the End of the World
for Jack, from Cape Espichel, Portugal

Unsuccessfully Africa barely invisible
memories piled stone and crenellated
vista after vista reaching where it
almost lurks at distant grey edge

Having come without names speaks
as best flat earth allows what danced
as Sirius's dark twin dances
still beneath saint's body sailed
from Valencia and planted
here upholding an idea
of recent rockets' glare
yet to be sailed around

Flashes of sun plunge to wince
whipped sea, last rocks, then Gloucester
Henry never went though driven
ship after ship against its
endless edge, south and south
till circumscribed caravans erased
in vast gathered wealth spelled end
of school's basking in talk of
Sirius's cool light, Al-Gharb
hot baked earth and palm's shade

Bent sextant to yearning
rocks, another school, and wind rose
whose use imagined, so spread
no bloom to love, blown extending lines
out, roads of known use
speaking saints' names over
and over till crows mock back
in black humour

Now beyond ruined Espichel
700 years also known as death
of Grail, tumbled arcade reeking
of piss, hellish slum corridor
greeting centuries' pilgrims –
beyond round white dome
rocks' edge, blue tile skull thoughts
barred against merely curious –
simple piled stones (grew once in a glass)
here and there, blue and red, (faces), up
slowly out of, A to B, or that twin again
still sleep, though tossing, then sea

Dislocation Flutter

Whatever the thought of that place here's where
contingent rocks utter coldly of old
wars fled and the edge of some leashed blood
still damp and running a course determined
in distant laboratories of discontinuous flows

Gone a shining button unknown
among clatter, dirt and grease, rolling
bones in doorways out a bus window that
marks an edge only words have crossed
on their way to on their way, past that last sign

Here is not gone though gone is this
twenty-foot plot at the boundary of a sentence
stretching from Pecos to defect beyond which
marauding Americans exact agency and
fragrance of hot granite and scorched grass

When I woke I was here, ductile sirens
wailing for demon lovers in streets beyond
whatever last page had been a metaphor
meant to suggest when the letters were big
and alive with a flutter aspens know in the wind

Caught between knowing the loss of
invisible dead chatter from dark
corners of star-fuckers and far-flung nets
and some lingering ache the flesh to be seen
to be reckoned in eye's hardening sweep

When I woke I was gone and the cypress
lined boulevards and faded stories rolled up against
the surf, the OK Corral and chiselled stones
the names no one there knows now all those
cars whipping past in heat and grey air

Catching the drift bends wind to an east
of blue through packed syllables threatens
fleshed edge of chaos scrawls some dim name
in scramble of forbidden transport to a sudden
human already north of where as other than gone

Off in Wittgenstein's Kitchen
A little post-apocalyptic suite for R.C. with thanks for the rhino

I

Endless plunge into precipitations
of density no wise predicted in white
recurring forecasts of post-holiday expulsions

beyond seasonal consolations racked up
in constant divisions and bullet-shattered
need for that jacket or just some vague

top-heavy knowing ever denied finally
even trumped-up vestiges of
magnificat fallen from the table

we scurry beneath having forgotten
where it's going or why it wants
us bewildered and refolded in blunt

intimations daily waiting a squeak
and rustle announces postman
deliveries of cheap drug and hardware flyers

2

Sudden precipitation of white
rhino in moment of revisionary push
past recurring forecasts of post-holiday

seasonal convulsions racked up
in constant division and bullet-shattered
need for that jacket or just some vague

top-heavy knowing assures it. What's not
in the room's on its way home, wired for death
denied even trumped-up vestiges

having forgotten where or why it wants us
daily waiting a squeak and rustle announces
postman deliveries of cheap drug and hardware

flyers slipped through the door it wrecked, pissed
off and headed out. There is no big white
rhinoceros in this plane reassures it

3

OK, the plunging's out. And that lovely vista
in spite the room it wasn't in. The rhino's
on its own, angels' hands, cushioning

the fall, the ways it's just there, so close
to the edge of the beat and the dirt
in your face. Having been snuck

up on, the floor tilts as it tosses
in drugged sleep beneath our feet
How did it get here through all that snow

and what's plunging got to do with it
when it's here? The angels' hands
a necessary rigour of the equation

claims plunges to keep its place
though it can't go back a sentence
no longer at home to it

4

Listen to it now, rustle, squeak
the same delivery, that plunge
branch to branch, and dirt

in your face doesn't wait
for thought of the common heart
to seal it. Mood a start or strut

as the whim on Emerson's door
shakes and rattles. Quote this and you're off
the team is all the room it leaves

barely enough for a white rhino
much less angels' hands out of
nowhere just as the branch

cracks and postman deliveries of cheap
drug and hardware flyers flutter
through plunges and slot to floor

5

At least the squeak can hold that worse than
death sung to sleep in a matter of
months, the moons slipping its metric

waking to pale thought in cat's eye
away. We may call it white
rhinoceros because it crashed

in the door of its use
and they shipped it back, though how
it got in here accounts the tale of one

too many sudden uses, as if you
thought to grab it but it was there
anyway, sitting at the table and

the tea, already cold to its rage
could not hold it up, however wired
from crucial tears of knowing

6

with apologies and thanks to Octavio Paz

Sometimes you get there and sometimes
the there gets you, a simple fact of how
turns it, a space of shifting constellations

at war with the mill. Unspoken animal
transpositions are not uncommon in this open
hand though whatever longing for manifestation

pieces together some verbal analogy
wrested (wrestled) from *imminence of a hymn*
recalls a certain precipitating density

threatens to devour these prospects
and any misplaced creation claims
the den or lair (lyre) in which not the there

but its displaced space stands up and shuffles
a familiar soft-shoe right out the wings
and into the arms of another blank page

7

Delirium of the alchemy of the word
HD's bitter crucible writ large and white
snorting around the edge of muddy

tracks emerged from flurry of frozen
densities in a pang barely known
beyond it. The thing is (or some other

gathering meets in unexpected space
to govern itself as if we could know
it asleep on the grate or its hand out

to our passing. They all want to know
how it got here, as if that passing
was not enough, as if this claim

on its hand was based on other than
Jack's *pan-axial encyclopedia proposition*
popped up in this morning's vacant blue passion

8

Black retinal letters etched in light across
familiar dark folds are *another place*
a rustle and squeak at the door of once

x'd plunge recurs without mercy
after a fit of revisionary
pique prompted in that other's silence

whence the rhino now presumably home
as plunge itself now seeks a rose
in it. Forget resistance and watch

it trot through the sentence they couldn't
kill in it, a kind of big white deferred
inflection whose corrosive decreation

leaves in its wake opportunity
otherwise lost to thinking the children
of music should win in place of the job

9

Pronounced elevation of mood by whom
founded the plunge and returned to angels'
hands via nuncio jacked up with straight

shots of light to the eyes adrift in buzz
of scriptural tombs and martial order
of reasons in shambles and scraps of its

logics even cheap drug and hardware
flyers can't diminish though blank
blow of that rustle and squeak shimmies

the works and knowing we're another
place so even return slips into
gerundial grinder as *plain you and*

me rides for its worth all that wonders
when to stop as opposed to say a white
rhinoceros wired for death and heading home

Equinotica

No wonder these fuzzy edges when
fire lurking in trees' hearts busted out
last night and that cold, promiscuous

clarity promising thoughts of moon's still edge
in tuned primordial gash through intersecting
assassinations, auroral intercessions

wild arctic dreams cut loose to dance
northern pole lost finally in blur
seen by Emerson in commercial prospects

rumble in morphic frenzy unflooding
improbable morning's new South African
vote two pages away from never having

thought how they suck entire dead season's
CO_2 in sudden transcending toke
hungry for it after unformed

secret of our lurching proposition
towards unexpected neighbours out of an
arduous story butting against other

streets filled with lines of hope, fine white
drift of scattered petals between us
radiant disaster triumphant

The Dawning of an Aspect

You're on the Earth, there's no cure for that.
– Samuel Beckett, *Endgame*

Strange that *piss* and *urination* thing
how they still fix some old fight
and memory of blue faces into
a proper post-Copernican distance
filled with permission to check your limbs
and organs at wit's end and get on with
business or war as usual

         I guess
it's the way that invasion itself feeds
some other need, or that old loss of body
pours into a story the guys whose arms
it filled probably didn't see given
flurries of arrows or hunger or death
of words now fallen into this starchy
white cure

        Or at least the thought of that
a kind of expanse, scarred but intact
free of terror, for which the charge is
measured in thousands of pounds, children's
bodies, a waking into a sleep of
ended explanations stopped dead in
the very knowing how to go on
could get us to that *diurnal devotedness*
that liberty come to us from
a rumoured distance

The same one in fact
that road in Jack's 'Homo Americanus'
caught between home and campsite (or just sheer
speed) runs through bent and twisted to the pull
of moon and sun that still *rise and fall*
in some unsettled translation
of Ohio that's truly a home of the free
unafraid of these little lists, demands
for marinades and horn relays played out
in day's familiar rush to a kind of end

Not of passion and certainly
not words, but sinking into
an old chair resonant now with
sounds of flesh from back before
it lost its untroubled surface, its thought
of home in the cold turbulent greys
of water and sky pound against
broken stones of this difficult shore

Solstique

Dark light flashing over wooden
ground beats out, even here, behind porous
fences, pain brings them out to sleep in banks

dreaming of bills out the walls they haven't
numbers for. Here it is highest and
still and what we have in its arms

reassures only faintly this wind beyond
us still breathes it. Who would have thought
the sun could stutter? Here it is high

and turning through lost drift of petals
pink and white in scattered pools reaching
for that blaze through dark fight flashing across

wooden ground unknowing what leaves them thus
dreaming, curled against the clatter. A burden
of light bound to drooping air whose here

ticks it off in a passage of shadows
past all thought of home turning mute dreams
awash in still moments mutter intolerant heat

Dancing in the Dark

Beyond the pale of Fred Astaire against
the evil empire where that electro
magnetic love thing and the counter
swing (it's those wild feet) does catch us in the weight

of ice and camellias as if it weren't
out there at all, though each of us then our
own comrade with Walt on that 'hill' so that silk
stockings lured Cyd Charisse over the wall

no longer command armies and lead us
not into redemption but dismantle
very machine renders invisible
all words recent emergent properties

of catacoustic *celestial mania*
ringing in the touch of first light brushes
this 'a,' that 'c,' still fires Bob's *small facts*
built from house of our *one unto one unto*

After Pieces Again
for R.C.

A given portion of matter consists, not of an individual portion of æthereal or other substance, but of modifications of the structure or energy or other qualities of the æther, and when matter moves it is merely these modifications of structure which are transferred from one portion of the æther to another.
     – C.V. Burton

here, it
calling it
structure as wave to sea
it
zone of slip

•

live here, æther
zone of slip
abuzz

•

sweep the floor it
's dirty
bring it back
bring it back

•

it's swelling
and it smells
of camellias
zone of slip
tunnelling

•

white tin
revealed hillocks
etched dislocation

•

hearing her it's
the whorl crystal grows
along (it's been done)
no, among

•

it doesn't get
any further
it doesn't
get

•

resisting mechanism
dislocation motion
the works along
a tunnelling
kink pair

•

say page and then
say home, say
it with feeling
zone of slip
it's said

•

tunnelling towards a whorled
image, rock
says it
approaching buzz
scrawl

•

if knock on wood's
as good in a pinch
where's the wood

•

would
that I could

•

shriek of fracture
walks a laugh along
simple fact
of dislocation

•

to another along
attractor pull
zone of slip?

•

William James said it's
memory and habit
hold it to
lattice emissions

•

the basement wall
crumbles it
forgot to dodge
gliding edge
dislocation

•

in light of dull
equinox, dark brush
of its other name

•

remember to look
both ways both
ways
knock on would

The Colour World of Birds

Earth is that very sun.
– Michel Serres

Add a fourth receptor and it seems all
heaven breaks loose, iridescent starlings
in angelic splendour, the whole thing there

all along as we've known at least since
heavenly blue and pearly gates of that time
now rushed to slam shut, recruitment

at the heart of chaos on the run
to some heat death filling sluggish
hunger huge boat plowing Pleistocene

waters Ellen dances in edge of screams
sheer noise grinds away at whatever closeness
to be found in frontier of fact at morning

glory. Never enough's name burning
net of lack, no way back's doom throttle's
singular roar sends it crashing this shore

we wind up, heated skin and sound of it
fading through sudden thoughts of Harvey and Jack.
Such dislocations flesh bears bobbing

in surge of waves rush towards other
ends than remains ice dumped here
holds us up yet against that push

Signs of Passing
for Amelia

I

If hot granite smells through rattling birch
memory of all that ice, is it any
wonder how this sweeps through her
waves, she said, as if you walked into the sea
itself a certain vibration and this
registration, a near translation, say,
hosannah or holy shit as the whole
works gears up for some chrysalis
nostalgia a name the last angel rolls up
and pulls out while light flickers in the branches

2

for Norma Cole

Anticipation is empty of silence
and the face in the mirror of these weathers
Who will come names every creak and leaf
as obliquities of puckered skin tell
ways through large and small catastrophes
Catasters the poet called her tossed words
and I heard cata-strophes, the unnerved
gesture in line's turn towards again not
as water utters against rocks though out
the unhinged windows what music does
lift its feet among suddenly scattered
syllables, cast stones along familiar verge

3

What's turned, turning down a father road
Farther. Ha. That knot of dropped 'r's and orphans
loosed upon the stretch of list. Difficult
belief, suspension of evening sky
in all prepositions at the lurch
unable to get any more reparable
than middle distance alight in cloud's
singular hanging, mere wisp of a world
Father road returns, sober if not straight
to speak of justice and allegiance in
Nordic bridge stretching from darkness to
darkness across all play of light and
water intoxicates fluoresced eyes

4

Shaken fodder by large winds enough
to rattle an overhead lost otherwise
to meaning business. Lost becomes one choice
after another, and coming back a chance
encounter. Feed me to it. Where it leaves
you have to begin, as if it weren't fall
or self-devouring words didn't vanish
before your knees gave out. Such a glance
constitutes a new nation, a notion
a small flutter in liquid fields of sound

5

How long can you leave it as question shifts
within this fear. The substance of her
body as it passes through unspeakable
complexities of flesh dissolves that too
brings it back in to particular nerve, pain
along a path only recently
introduced to memory's pleasures, call
it xanadu or habit, and wind up
in any case, in Thoreau's backyard, such
as it is, those scraps of a shack. This
inhabitation and its swells of new
knowing whisper even over here old
words of what that teaching means that, dark
massive, settles into an arrangement
of æthers we can almost recall

6

,

Silk to spider hauls in the trembling at
edge of nadir of some post-cosmological
bounce looks a lot like dragging Emerson's
yea into compulsory sentencing's
fear of the dark they sleep in, almost hum
of creation's fleshy tumult above
talking heads of why they lock up all those
black men under cover of soul's dark night
as hummingbirds weave silk homes, small cups
from species unknown to science. Offer
gifts, wild turkey and weed till banished saints
sneak back to tame that wild night, though utter
density of not so much the flesh as
a kind of floating edge dislocation
through knowledge growing rounder still hums
overhead, sucked into ancient
habits we drift placidly behind

7

Bearing in mind it into this war our
way out beyond any easy turn down
some syntax set to old music's ability
to still a racing heart, even within
darkness prepares fiery letters' home to
write its house, its name already turning
not here, but in sudden stops and starts it
all turns to, even this 400-year
old mean streak masked behind light bulbs and
better as if it wasn't noise of that
beating itself, thumping coil woven
around nothing's knot stands eventually
face to face with blow or embrace so that
they, too, swing, and the poem murmured
into flesh its dwelling mingles among
voices of all those busy pumps to speak
those dazzling feet never quite touch the ground

8

So maybe Einstein's got his answer now
it just keeps heading out, Baudrillard's
precession setting up shop in the Kali
Yuga's *terrain vague* out in that strip
mall on 7. Hell, somebody's got to
do it, but what kind of assurance works
when even poets don't know a mock
heroic from a non-referring hole
in the ground. Whence autochthonous *tickled pink*
rises from some stratum of grandmotherly
bugs' ears and hollow legs to mind again
this longest dark and its turnings, old love
back to flame's coded poinsettias, that spark's
elusive and nagging chuckle beyond
any end's doom of our frightened making

9

In air again, traversed edges of vague
wars, negotiated boundaries past
any school of thought strangers murmur home
of white ground when thinking Uganda
because it says so and probably not
knowing Apollo's sheep before escaped
gas beyond flimsy walls and other tales
of melted wings. Together is just
such a rag-and-bone operation you'd
think world's turning in darkness would hold
us to, just the other side of parodic
gestures hoping to turn us from all that
white-knuckle business, but then cling to
unable to release projective this
or that and get on with it, they call it
a Perilous Voyage thinking the moon's
other than here's further and death's different
than laughter, itself then a rock and those
chains it thought to burst another name
for hunger brings it back day after day

Call it the retardation of lunar
momentum and it just might get past
whatever cross-legged imposition
remains of the Grand Tour's breathless legacy
to this room, a shifting of planetary
mass within whatever sentence remains
to be served, as if a certain inflection
could budge here's seeming stall beyond, no, in
to perhaps resistance hunt-crazed women
of Thebes knew belongs to us all, even
here, midnight, the kitchen now a name
of consequence, maybe that's what Jack meant
not the story itself or accumulated
decor but the charge those incursions
stutter of, that bloody death of the
innocent still murmurs from the dead
of love as the other side of the
boundary of lost possibility

11

The surprising coincidence of nine's
ripening turn and year's own term runs off
at right angles to any premature
correspondence of tenor's vehicular
departure to parts known in white blur's
demand for attention, the usual
suspects, or sus*pects*, in which case
domesticated returns to mystery
of its own unsuspected corners, dark
and baffling as any Mexico in
the cupboard, especially that swelling
no amount of dead subjects (*Madam,
perhaps you haven't heard that in Casablanca
life is cheap*) or abandoned
summa summarum to yet another
cheap parodic laugh can possibly hope
to escape except that leap from the window
out the kitchen and into the cold
relish I hadn't meant to arrive at
though I guess coming down to that beat
always leaves us face to face, even now
to flesh's nested circulations

12

No matter how you try to go around that 'water'
backed against any damn thing you'd care
to say, quotes or any other inflection even
some quotidian dado might bear from insistent
contact with fractions and angles on interpretations
of water leading irresistibly back to a first
poem in a strange land not withstanding,
it's still the name of that swelling in lilac's
tough tips out of ice, previous coincidence
impervious to any now discounted penetration
of eternity hard against count's strictures, the whole thing
stretched nearly past bearing as if flesh were metaphor's
last stand, home to errant swans on the lam
resistant not just to absorption but that refusal
of inside out's turning and pushing stretches
her belly into miraculous, alien form promising
to release us into *ten thousand virgin eyes'*
drunken blows against sudden rush of wings

Mabonesque

Still whatever curl the telling sun beats
against, whatever fruits and grain
conjured brain buttresses in such remorse

whips across haphazard lake out of what
we really know and into those lights
along an edge extends further than

thinking its connections alone in the dark
undreamt deposits thrust sparkling
out of surrounding cloud where sounds of

slaying death and Corn-wolf lurking
in the final sheaf speaks 'wolves' and leaves
us there where voices drift over water

beats on stones dumped from endless excavations
displaced loaves still borne in sleep to wreak some
peace from utter hurt, hot sidewalks for

pillows turned cold and damp, translated
into equally days desperate
lengthened shadows eking out what sense

each rite of thanks seems to have seen before
in burning bodies dot this day's casual
learning from ruined remains of cast lots

Interlude: Ode to the West Wind
for Schrödinger's cat

O, a world, red, brown, and cat
in the grass, twisting willow space along
some Queen's way, over
arched or arc, arcadian glare
to archaic intent emerged
from thick grey covering cherub
notes lake within lake, there along
dimly cold and blue ruined wave
now given to road's tawdry decor
because a world it doesn't buy

Try telling them 'a' and 'o' or wheels
songs Walt wrote while one-winged
birds flutter blankly down leaves
of unspelled pages longing till it's all
so dull even light's collapsed curve
of possible cats slinks back through
daunted fence into the box of its
sea blooms and oozy woods, bereft
though certainly game, still

Counting out nine while leafless
revelations, meagre yellow remnant
flapping loose G-string, unexpected
sounding note through same bare
geometry beyond photos, plants
stacked boxes surprised
by begets and dragged towards naked
unwelcome allegory wrapped around
a pole lost in brown alley's distant

Stairs where up to the wall and then
there is genius, dark secret twin again
where else the breath of autumn's
dim verge, devoured words for angel's
room, tutelary twigs clicking against
walls, teeth, inspiration
swells and rattles and clicks on driven
to pluck at what thin tubular
remains yet hang and knock and bang

Reunion

If Guinevere and Lancelot met again
at the mute grey roof of the world

while the engine ran and the sky fell
gathering inside to fog whatever distance

they had built of silence and sheer
accumulation of minutes full of shopping

and comic postures, other loves and laundry
till mountains that may or may not

have floated in light at sky's edge
once every hundred years almost meant

enough to explain youth in occluded
perspectives, properties of horizons

within which the tattered rose named Rhonda
or Compassion, a bit brown around

frosted edges but red for all those weathers
did not lurk in mists closed in to leave them

stunned and stuttering, a sad joke
face to face with knowing that cruel

perfection of the heart that once
every hundred years rises luminous

and exact in the throat and burns
fugitive eyes flick wildly within sudden

density of attenuated years now thick and damp
upon the dark glass they flutter against

The Name of Bone

If I stepped into the pool your eyes of it left
adrift in its sky, blue and vast though
perhaps betrayed by a flutter at the edge
of that sudden stillness (*turning
to reach for the missing bag*) what could it say?

Each life we leave loves on till that overcast
day a door opens and it leans out smiling
the price of words scrawled in rock, screech
of crystal dislocations across blackboard
souls of chalked names and possible homes?

Some shift in the system's buzz, a tweak
out of nowhere and the whole enchilada – well
say it wasn't thirty years or we hadn't tossed
in our hands when death came to play, what then
the price of peering down the arch of your throat?

The insubstantial body caught in these periodicities
of elemental interruption loses its place and sets
up near hinged edge of an old ache where having
been left behind keeps house in the blaze
flickers the untended blow of your glance

The trick turned in sweet time to speak
of hope leaves before getting caught
with its pants down, longing simply for
a moment unburdened by roaring engines
running on empty and that old rocky lure, to hear of you?

To take it just past there to some new habit
of stars adrift in the wind and untold
encounters in flush of again, and if you, looking
deeply into this ragged impossibility, glanced
away, isn't this the indigestible name of bone?

Then ribbed estuarial fading into sea's
memory of lilacs or some wild groping
amidst the grove next to the mill just beyond
where the house burned down and the station
moved on leaving drowned gestures to float away

Scattering States

Just past the burnt landscapes across all
thought of willows, the wild residuum
at edges in each arch and wave far north

of any creek of rare trees in sandy bottoms
almost word-like, as who remembers their
own first speaks to its filling our mouths

and leaving us to banks of cloud blow in
after sixteen long days, no rain
forests further up burning with fury

here is now immune to other than
news zooms us in and out, low over
muted images can't speak news of

lobelia blue ravaged eyes at edge of
any thought of home anticipating
constant evacuation, even

here in this garden amidst arching
grasses, common nameless graces, not so
much out of fear, just that pressure of rain

to wash away whatever scattering states
across parched ground leaves us always just this
side of already broken and on our way

So They Say

Thinking Jerusalem's terror against a stiff, wet wind, early
March till caught in tall, brunette gaze and world's tumble
into a common grace of ruins at corner of another age

old answer and now returns to deserted motels, last days
of legendary bars, and everywhere the fungus glow
holding in thrall where it was. Then suddenly passing

stillness into foliations of eyes, extensions of limbs along
vortex of unleashed patterns of wind and sky. Is that the face
of anyhow nothing personal intended but the constant

wreckage congealed in random people reading of money
as if it marched across the sky like a finger
anæsthetized upon a billion minds? Kissing off all those

dollars for the simple thought of America's floating
shores – what the hell is a cobble, anyway, after eleven
years in Buffalo? – impossible commensuration always

just beyond your hometown, not to mention Stein's
country, twitching like a wired frog's leg or the refracted
light around the riveted wing of cinderella each of us harbours,

an entry dazzling suddenly in unexpected dance of talking
in the solarium. How can I remember the random elevation
of scullery maids when falling behind otherwise words

from the carpet of clouds. Ah, time, that canary clime
we come to on the unshored shore of an approaching
sea, watching from the northern extension of a heart

tenderized by love's mallet, syntax beckons, past how do you
say the expected lame greeting dictated in an after stitched
together beyond these hobbled walls of grounds and terrors

Golden Chersonese

The actual shape of it through whatever grind –
six the clock, seven the *Globe*, eight Sally, and then and then
along an ex and why, any point, though usually
the kitchen at some other six, sesame oil, garlic,
Amelia, the history of barbed wire, as someone
said, my wife
                                    If you don't get it, it gets you
having to eat the mode of stillness within growl
and clank of collection days a taste for stones
betrays, tooting any way it pleases you it's still
dusty and claims an arrangement of all
todays until they're gone wherever
                                    The work
of entering it lost as Jack's *three*, a pearl world
like Colon saw to the south, Solomon's *Golden
Chersonese*, heavenly earth, though that already gone
to mammon as we see even what scraps left
cut down for the pennies to be had, all that shadow
going around and now it seems coming
up the walk, rattling the door, testing
windows
                                    Absent the mysterium of the exit, if only
as limit makes tune's passage, what's left nothing
but a weak typology of mythic goods, heroic
Coke versus Pepsi some legendary
residue, classic at that, though as usual
name sucked dry just when it might get you up
for fight now faces with nay, with no longer
even a car to speak of down that tree
corridor, though come to think of it
beer's getting good again after all that
Americanization, might be some shift
in the buzz calling poets home from
equals to a further responsibility, legislation
returned disequlibrium of coastal reflection
along fractal edge, a balance

Through

You could say they were *lives*, feathers
incidence of reflection along a breath
(that attention gone to the dogs
of connection
                        Of course we live there and of course
Sonny Bono slammed into a tree five days
after Michael Kennedy snapped his neck
in same digression
                        How you do it is you go
one CV, two a job, three scanning the stuff
salvaged from crashed hard drive, four
read 'Tlön, Uqbar, Orbis Tertius,' five call
Victor, you know the drill
                        You could say
they were feathers or iron, that greeny flower
out of some unnamed mode of progress unfolding
not towards light bulbs but vibration itself a
procedure of cause if we take into account
quantum action at a distance

Seven on the Bay

1 Enormous Bodies of Water

to have done nothing
is perfect
    – William Carlos Williams

Who it is thinks gifts while dreams of searching
small red shrooms among wild strawberries lounges
on the deck won't slip into what seemed its
sense of allegorical responsibilities
remain the former property of
communicable relations now that
shoe don't fit. Thick band of heat hugging
colder currents liberates white fins to
the sun, a secret of hulls, a contracted
hush of faded hulls over deep cold currents
will not mean this day after it's turned loose
among angels of evaporation. Still
it says it even as Brownian motion
of molecules excites senses to
extravagances of vision among
glacial ghosts and beginning to slip into fog

2 Heaven

The bleat the bark bellow and roar
Are waves that beat on heaven's shore.
  – William Blake

If you rate it on basis of pure
liquidity, light no doubt takes
cake given matter and all that

business, though Saturday's *Globe*
carries quantum news of effects
at distances and speeds beyond even

light's former limits and passing
through obstacles as only
numbers can leaves no bounds

to tie us down to that back
to back business, no explanation
other than twin star action as

Jack saw in Dogon's Sirius stuff
dark twin still being writ here
where he witnessed the boat

go over, later managed to get
right side up in this local
directional pocket we call home,

that too elsewhere's news by piled rock
pit for fire, glaciers so close
water still smells of them, scaring off

casual swimmers from the
south, gesture of stones night
feeding at edge of flickering light

maybe that's what they meant by
heaven, light's name whispered
voice of water and stone

3 This Aversion
for Dennis from Georgian Bay

Lying in the beds we've
    made vibrates with waves
        of churning quickly through

dark matter

residue of less
    domestic lives still
        haunts shadows of

birch grove –
    these stones, myriad
        detritus of stacked

and shattered æons infolded
    prints of small alien lives
        will not speak their names

to answer libations or other
    defunct gestures of abjection

        nor welcome the stranger among
his alien words and their
    obscure paths always
        lead just here – dumb

ghost of some glacier
    offering indecipherable
        hieroglyphs to ferment in the sack

earth and sky we're charged with
    brewing in teeth of nomad
        night's lament

4 Les vertiges des grandes intimes

The dream is not bawdy. It is something else.
– Ludwig Wittgenstein

Seven a.m. sun and birch shudder within Amelia
tangled already in white caps race across world's blue face,
pomegranate secret structure as opening to
Hariot's gaze a world of boundaries and imperfections
la belle noiseuse prying open each moment to loose clouds
across scree of morning's tangled edges reading here
breaches limits of tales to hold together these
interruptions lost amid conveniences of mortality

First the vowels and labials splashed across random
distances half embraced in jerking arms bent to half-formed
intent. If it doesn't stick, the glue's no good, though of course
I don't mean glue, I mean lake before written, a stillness
interrupted only by monied guns own the island
across the water. Even there, and the street, empty
image palace stripped bare – if it's not the stories' doing
is it democracy, that weird exhalation of Detroit?
Or pink lights behind cheap Deco fixtures? Call this stiffened
blush engorgement of the edge in an impossible
series of impaired connections to her smile

The yet-to-be-dreamt names of bears being no cheap trick
bringing those waters in neither as cycling
angels through first days refuse to move in, to settle so
even now passing shadow across ground or face
chill's sudden passage to same smile speaks tuning her soul not
as morning paper sells harmony to faint of heart,
magnetic north to random terror of hard-won noise
but a ruffling across those waters of limits as friends
mark the boundaries we know

5 A Visit

One of those old marvels
still occasionally given
to find us in
stepwise and expanding
attending unexpected there
at another one – levels
aside, and up and down,
say, into and out, unfolding
seduction, whatever gorgeous
or self-sufficient given precisely
towards conversion, turning
around who speaks from
ripples umber oil
across blue ebony lake skin

6 Interrogative

Cupped in hands
does it answer
the moon as mind
in bay holds it
to stony shore against
slaps and whispers of depths
eyes seek ranging ruffled
face springs to wind
out of west darkened
to sing it?

7 Excision of the Encephalon

So call it *oceanic feeling*, but that's still just a wall
something the Army Corpse of Engineers might throw up
along the Mississippi – wow, Canada just took
the 400-yard relay from the Americans –
to hold some ordered and stacked obedience, that one
over another we thought we'd left sometime
in the seventeenth century but still shows up to haul
the world in flopping and serve it up not even just
as a body which after all has access in its
recesses to memories of distances carbon
travelled after being forged in those old stars' hot hearts
and spewed out, but as if flesh had been mangled and
hung up to dry bereft of the solaces' figuration –
no, not just that but the pulse itself, so deep the morning
paper says Nicaraguan children have invented
language when none was offered, instinct the word now hides
in itself what we don't want to know about the tuning
of Amelia's soul, that same initiation leads
to Bamanan chief's sectioned skull through slow regulation
of rhythm's work across years towards *ataraxia*
otherwise known as *the ox* though democracy as we
have so far pitifully imagined its hobbled
lineations would probably confuse it with Prozac

The Execution of Karla Faye

Of course they've been cheering death forever, ask
Lorca or Antigone, an execution a day in the US
they say, something to work for, that guy in the Stop 'N' Go
when they bombed Gaddafi's kid, cheering at
the thought of pain, but that's the neighbourhood's
dark end anyway, get used to it, light your candles
march around the lake, don't lose sight of Amelia
(how they *ever* could have thought that smile less
than all their clutching – Wordsworth had that down
alright – then here we are, maybe that's what they hope
to drown out cheering the news she died when the state
whatever the hell that is plunged or pulled whatever *techné*
ecstasis extension holding it to crucial distance, still somewhere
flesh touches some thing, and we'd better be prepared
for the whole bloody mess because even if home
of ourselves is a rumoured *infrapsychisme* from which
undisputed program is accessible to, say, rejig the works
thru poem's possible modulations, there's still north
of that, south, east, west and when you get home
guess who's waiting

Solstique 2

*Men today are about 5'8" tall. Cro-Magnon cavemen from
Europe were six feet and had skulls with 10% more volume.
This last phenomenon is the most puzzling of all, for our
brains have been diminishing just as we have been embark-
ing on mental feats that have given us world domination.*
      – Globe and Mail, December 21, 1994

No puzzle there, the shrinking skulls a sure
sign of lost social reverberating
even then as if the ice itself marked

some edge of us adrift in blue
shifted streets tightening even as slant
of light utters diminished and final

gestures of completion in the heated
greenhouse shrinkage of what eager reaching
birthed out of the dark odylic night

muted anagogs we've run on since till
they stand on corners, hands out, cold and pale
to remind us commonly held dream binds

shambles we live in and knowing longest
of its nights still turns though now perhaps
towards unwalled adjustment out there where they

first thought that star if only we can find
a way to see through all this ambient
enlightenment without getting hung up

on literalized excretions we think
to extend precious hand only to find
ourselves squeezed in grip of our own

wanting from whose endless hole the missing
ten might be lured back here, low and cold
but bearing news the ice took with it

hHell

for bpNichol

You can't just pretend abrogating map
makers or any stripe of telling will pass
beyond grid's legation in a must
see it contracting, not, say, momentary
maple devag marking now springs to parry

but utter legibility burning bone brings
to season's legislative initiatives, some poet's
meagre prisoner – 'o' writ smaller even
than own brutal gesture's code made cellular
limits, little less polis's testament to eyes

would be direction a different zone
inframental single lone gunman's eye stops
at grassy knoll in an equal to very best
you've got to offer set a little apart
since at least Milton saw it brute and bloody

now exactly noise springs never
in visibly gratitude to Al's Mycenaean cows
across road, stripped of all protogonic
climates anticipatory to no more world's
extraordinary autonomy in lockstep

still in Kant's *dawn* around objections
to every move past insistent rabble's
mallet love bereft of god's arm meant it
an embrace equal to never
give a foot to no sucker sun till we

find out if mind and language finally
will play – call it America or Wal-Mart
stacks of equals in penny-counting days
and poet's down to precise
doesn't matter anyway under clamour's

lintel – but on alternate digits suppose
a mutt or an angel or
suppose vagaries of luminosity
in cellular skin, suppose out
of bounds, terminal variance as

an arrangement of roses and dandelions
suppose an abundant gesture
of windows, a word beyond its own word
suppose waves and particles at
marbles – locking up snug taxes and

skipping away could get you far
beyond a question of criss-crossed streets,
so far it all may equal zip-zip as slipping
into more comfortable digs its own
fragrance beyond any simple prescription

of democratic rules insistent
reduction to working stiff, cow's
taxonomical dead end in virtue's denial
of luxuriant street sign's odyssean
creation, and delivers not unto mere

baggage, but reminding mermaids along
Davenport's coastal, along coasting we've
always slipped into its *areality of ecstasy*
as protest set to lock down any works
drifts off towards its own sad reward

Next

for Liz

I

returned some quickened breath to round
of unexpected encounters, there
where gate's shadow falls coldly across
hard ground or here where the window calls back
untouched blue words, loose and rattling
whatever abandoned whim chooses
to bless you with sweet jackhammer songs
and screeching saws reach as a hand
out of a cloud, no, an image of a photo
of a drawing of an image of a cloud
there, off between the chimney
and that grey slant of roof it barely touches
in airy chimes around bright surface rings
some distant thought through thickened light to now

2

of unexpected encounters, there
seem to have been forgotten in another
phrase of blue, as if this was no less
than the sight of her, there at that gate
each night coming home. If it wants a certain
substance where it meant to go out and meet
her, out of control or knowing tomorrow
once the moon is over the edge, adrift
in her eyes, she'll bring it back and arrange
it in some dark corner otherwise lost
forever to careless, frightened
excesses and whatever days, cold
barren, but suddenly bright with that glow
hauls up the day and leaves it there afloat

3

phrase of blue, as if this was no less
a presence which practical operations
having led to neglect wants to go on
meeting there within a subverted
perspective. Which one don't you know and how
does it go on if you don't want to hurt
the variable distance? Like meat? She
won't eat anything with eyes doesn't help
analogous organizations, now
left behind the dust in a madness
gets you around Kant but smack up against
stench of that question they all think to say
as if *man* was enough in the crack of that
fading beast's all-too-leftover puzzle

4

meeting there, within a subverted
astonishment, the difficult kiss
stretched distance past all thought of home on down
that road at end of day returns it here
intervals' intensities relational
havoc erupting into errancies'
embrace, swinging gate at that edge of shade
from which knowing the next within its own
wish swerves into her arms even as stars
stare out at night's swirl and swish, still turned on
that fire lights within what orient I
think in scrambled skies, star to star to
trace what hot and fleeting hold had set that
limpid bear adrift to signal tender edge

5

intervals' intensities relational
moment, neither then nor then but how
her smile strips it of double while the wonders
about it goes on simply at ease
in a touching me, in a you are
as if that bay I enter stepping from
rock to rock through beyond clear resided
in a residual mobility
dreams speak between white birch circle and
all the way across that tossing water
Jack spoke through, no need of blood or threats
just a certain gap or gash as between
this grunt and the glint of her eyes in that
suddenly immense hold of its enigma

6

as if that bay I enter stepping from
each breath, each this to this along that curve
of scattered rock misled such errant
gestures skidded over the oozy top
of some sheer fact, displaced senses its
relational frenzy, unexpected
turns into her arms and then each day she's
there, at the end of thinking's stretch to take
its worth on home, agaric nimbus
derived from nothing to explain that queer
thing, that fire's breath of manifold virtues
stoop to heaven or some other face
rises sparks from burning birch a text
surprises each who come to read those flames

7

turns into her arms and then each day she's
next to impossible or beside its rage
at dinner, a curious turn that leaves
us wondering through densities thick
and distant, unexpected as a yellow
truck, face to face across that winding road
a crunch and pop and knowing then how next
it is, how hard to handle once the turn
is made though here it's shrine as well as where
light drifts across red asphalt tiles in late
afternoon, fugitive and common
as a sudden rush of cool air across
hot words stalls and pauses in the silence
brooding in reluctance pools behind it

8

it is, how hard to handle once the turn
next to the thought of you has been made,
no matter of blown candles or gestures
otherwise lost to its daily bread,
a question of finding the words where they
lurk in the folds of that day and call it
out, say to play or maybe to fish
each line bent sharply there where it enters
this murky business, ending in whatever
intense purposes come up for some air
laughing at tangled limbs and determined
unions in spite of the brutal engine
and absent roses to penetrate
I that I sees you there out of that cloud

9

this murky business, ending in whatever
conclusions reach out and touch the difference
between tottering stacked books register
a mess of bifurcating paths that lose
and find a way through unforecasted rage
pressed and folded in neat piles as if that
simple description touched exact spot where
some other world in just its own image
a latent disturbance moving out
of the north, dark and flashing, shone through it
or lost it in an unsuspected maze
contained within the sentence erupted
its own business all over the room
otherwise given to predictable

of the north, dark and flashing, shone through it
with next to nothing and her sudden calm
a furious reminder of its turn
down those other avenues we hadn't
occurred in, a bull in the field and some dead
guy for reasons impossible to get
together or away from all these years
later when it pops up before departing
for that old place, suddenly silent and
blank in the nexus of simultaneous
provocations continuing echo
terminal moraine of Dogtown's solid
rock still there whispering through passages
lead to that gate swinging in sun and dead leaves

provocations continuing echo
in liberty's non-conclusive embrace
establishes premises beyond your
wildest dream's itinerant longings for
simple down-home pleasures, knowing that next
to *her*, or *next* to her, in any case
knowing the distance between here and
dominion in the building of it, dead
reckoning Thoreau said as if heaven
too was a matter of how you managed
that dying we lose in meat and shiners
for perch when only attending to each
star will do where choosing arrays itself
in figures flicker over the heart's vault

12

I did not own
even the gesture my hand was
made of
     – Asa Benveniste

for perch when only attending to each
hold as for your life won't do but how
else go on when it starts writing a you
that wasn't next, that wasn't even then
and won't take its teeth out of your throat for
any proverbial recourse appeals
to rags and bones of what mattered when it
first dreamt you then left you hanging to squawk
at cruelty of the heart's perfection
never stops wanting who looked out next
to you over the river from Brooklyn
or Zion as the boat named America
and the whole thing, lost to some sudden
dictates of uncompassed ruptures and home

13

and the whole thing, lost to some sudden
next to a wall or the end of the line
that blank, say, space? That arrested silence
clamouring in margins of an instance
plays out the dream of meant to be
where meaning's quarrel with wrecked heart
of being leaves us aghast at sheer
mean resistance to knowing the further
self of its own tender proposal, its
sweet wish of skin and skin as if marriage
were to write there at the edge of a hot
breath stone's answer to the very question
no one asked it before moving on to
unravelling limits irreparable

14

unravelling limits irreparable
drift thusward to what trembling registers
faint and insistent beyond that gate's
gaping specificity, click of feet
coming or going at the edge of night's
embrace promises any case you might
think watching the thief of instincts stroll by
on his way to coffee or fame while clothes
tumble in the dryer beneath this floor
and history twists in the wind rattles
deadened chimes and scatters news across
hardened white ground anticipating
some dark star's mute appeal via twinned
nimbus to the exposure of that next

Dislocations of Crystal

Out where sun's a point of view wheels
squeal against the glare, the impossible
turns beneath clean, clear America

that yet uncommon sky possessed unfinished
names beyond no further *fire in the belly*
of irreducible four or six is

yet there: to speak for itself of babble's
ear incomplete year turning derailed
rhymes into baffled whether's precipitate

beyond, white names we wake to any
day mumbled against the jazz or news that
hauls us back and dumps us stuttering

of groceries and blood, adrift where home
itself's alone and waking to Bing's
hallelujah, our *facilities of*

locomotion lay bare. Sitting there
dead smile from frames and rolling worlds
gather steam returning gesture's bone

to a bit of warming ground that same
sun now heats to root and thrust against
immobile lattice lap whose dislocation

begins in groan or gleam in which her human
(strange as strange flesh, somatic deformation)
displayed glass dance, hard and dark where it yet to

dance again and ends tomorrow. So near and yet
here, out on that road through north to stone
and home, her voice, that song to which the feet

Postlude: Ode to the New Year

No amount of road undoes
viral ravage of lost image though
some wet smile still reigns
in floral Columbus down distant
Pasadena street. Take it it's ours:
tobacco, chilis, tomatoes, even
lumpy potato later stuck
with eyes, mouths, hands
could winter underground
like some dim goddess
safe from ravaging bands
of hungry soldiers replacing
rye ultimately led to so many
damn people, consequent
machine now grapples and rips
whole trees from sucking
earth while we search
the map for 3 7 north

Turgid harvest waits intrepid
hearts, yawning white year
and Africa's twisting throes
laboratory death, lurid ivy
hung dream of skull
and bones democracy, legions
of plutonium salesmen
in the pasta mart. O Cristóbal
brief, cold flashes still lurk
between ragged split rail
geometry, tough stone harvest
drove farmers to night's
haunted whispers

Dead against text says however
edifying clings to surface, whirl
and eddy, Elvis at the minimart
telling knowing's edge at *gnar*
across pellicular expanse, *Egypt*
of distractions, Dealey Plaza, sheer
nilotic shallowness related flood
stories the whirl, Capt Picard against
a language of incident speaks
Gilgamesh across worlds' skins
as rising water resembles fire
mind sees in its own *histoire*
of the President's wife
scrambling after his head

What it is rises unanswered
to scintillant frozen forest standing
for fabled morals, thought through
with unfounded emerald flashes
towards no final rising nor *paradis*
des sauvages stammering out
fair-haired angel's dim tale
of another new world mistaken
again – Mr Potato Head risen
from cold ravaged euro-grave
across sun-crossed meridian
indicted course when looking north
from Shakespeare's bark
into morning's opaque shell

Acknowledgements

Some of these poems appeared previously in the following magazines and chapbooks: *Angle, Descant* (Ft. Worth), *First Intensity, Hambone, Phoebe, Skanky Possum, Talisman, The Germ, TO, Dislocation Flutter* (Oasii) and *Three Pellicular Odes* (shuffaloff).

Specific quotations and materials have been taken from Ralph Waldo Emerson ('Off in Wittgenstein's Kitchen' 5, 8, 9; 'Dancing in the Dark'), Octavio Paz ('Off in Wittgenstein's Kitchen' 6, 'hHell'), John Clarke ('Off in Wittgenstein's Kitchen' 7, 'This Aversion'), Novalis ('Dawning of an Aspect'), Robert Creeley ('Dancing in the Dark'), Stéphane Mallarmé ('Signs of Passing' 12), Michel Serres ('The Colour World of Birds,' 'Les Vertiges des Grandes Intimes'), Leo Bersani and Ulysse Dutoit ('Next' 4), Giorgio Agamben ('Next' 14) and Jean Francois Lyotard ('Dislocations of Crystal,' 'Postlude: Ode to the New Year').

And for – in varying degrees – their support, criticism and patience, my gratitude goes out to Robert Creeley, Robin Blaser, Cass Clarke and Elizabeth Brown – and to those *elsewhere* who continue to care.

About the Author

Michael Boughn is a writer, scholar and sometimes teacher. Previous volumes of poetry include *Iterations of the Diagonal* (shuffaloff, 1995) and *one's own MIND* (1999), the penultimate volume in *A Curriculum of the Soul* published by the Institute of Further Studies in Canton, NY. In 1993 he published *H.D.: A Descriptive Bibliography 1905–1990*. He is currently working on a bibliography of Charles Olson, a new book of poems called *Precarious Situates* and a second mystery novel called *Hornet Summer*. He lives in Toronto with his wife, Elizabeth, and their two children, Amelia and Sam.

Typeset in Sabon and Albertus
Printed and bound at the Coach House on bpNichol Lane, 2003

Edited by Darren Wershler-Henry
Cover painting by Lynn Donoghue
Cover design by Rick/Simon

Visit our website:
www.chbooks.com

Send a request to be added to our e-mail list:
mail@chbooks.com

Call us toll-free:
1 800 367 6360

Coach House Books
401 Huron Street (rear) on bpNichol Lane
Toronto, Ontario
M5S 2G5